creative fun with
plastic
bottles

By Nikki Connor
Illustrated by Sarah-Jane Neaves

An Aladdin/Watts Book

© Aladdin Books Ltd 1997

Designed and produced by
Aladdin Books Ltd
28 Percy Street
London W1P OLD

ISBN 0 7496 2711 5

First published in
Great Britain in 1997 by
Aladdin Books/Watts Books
96 Leonard Street
London EC2A 4RH

Design

David West Children's Book Design

Illustrator
Sarah-Jane Neaves

Photographer
Roger Vlitos

Printed in Belgium
All rights reserved

A CIP catalogue record for this book
is available from the British Library

Contents

Before you start

A "what you need" ingredients panel appears with the photograph of each project. Decide which project you are going to make and collect everything you need.

 The red, yellow and blue paint pots mean that you need poster paints. All colours (except white) can be made by mixing together a combination of these three. See the colour chart at the back of this book to find out how. You may choose instead to use ready mixed colours if you have them.

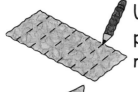 Use a pencil point to punch holes in paper or thin plastic. For thicker cardboard and plastic, you may need to use scissors - <u>ask an adult to help</u>.

 A dotted line in the instructions means you are to fold, not cut. A solid line shows where to cut.

Only use scissors that are especially designed for children's crafts. They usually have rounded ends. Always have an adult with you when you use them.

 Where a project needs coloured paper remember you may use any colour you choose. If you have none, use white paper and paint it!

If you follow the step-by-step instructions carefully you will be sure to finish up with a successful model - but if you prefer to use these designs just as ideas to get you started, then that's fine too!

Have fun.

skittles

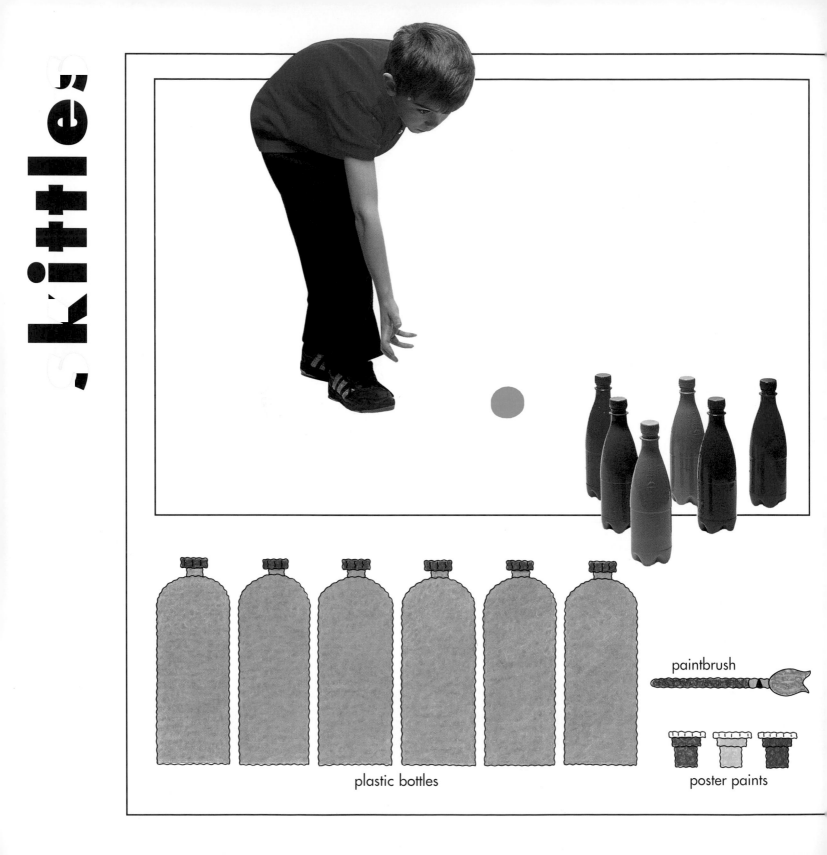

plastic bottles

paintbrush

poster paints

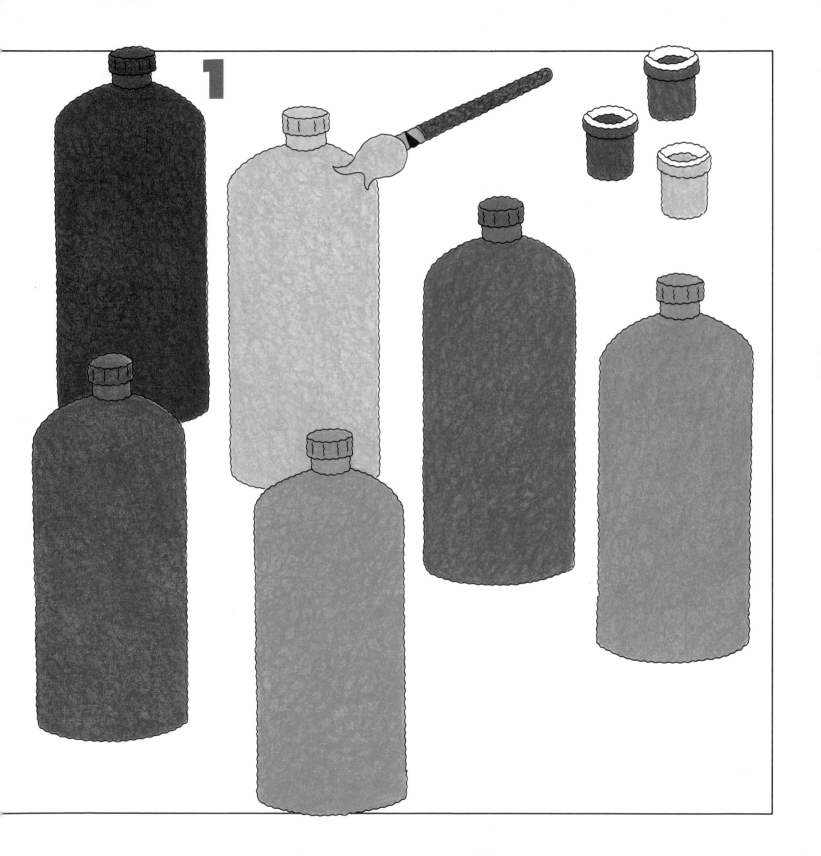

flowerpot

plastic bottle

scissors

paintbrush

poster paints

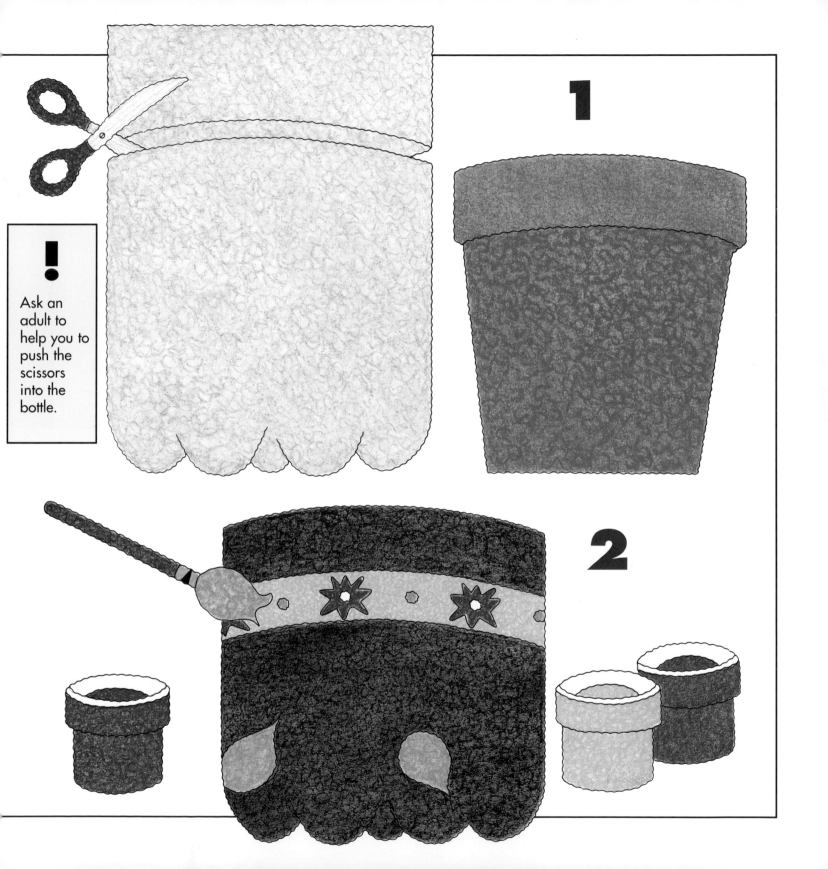

1

2

plastic bottles

wooden sticks

paintbrush

poster paints

rice grains

sticky tape

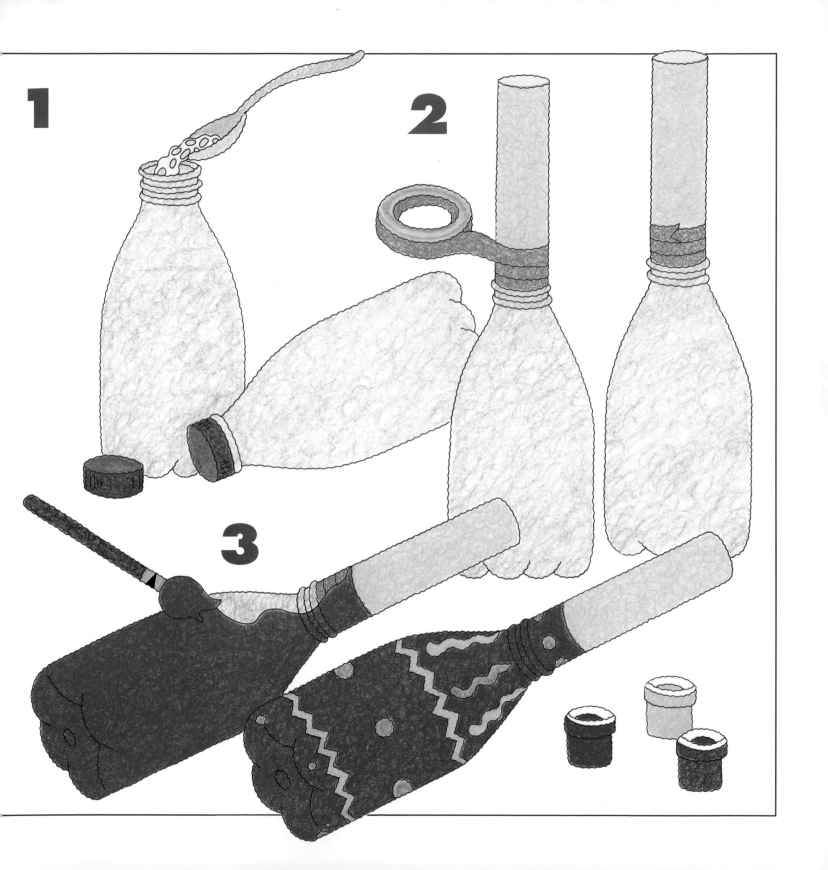

bangles

plastic bottle

scissors

paintbrush

poster paints

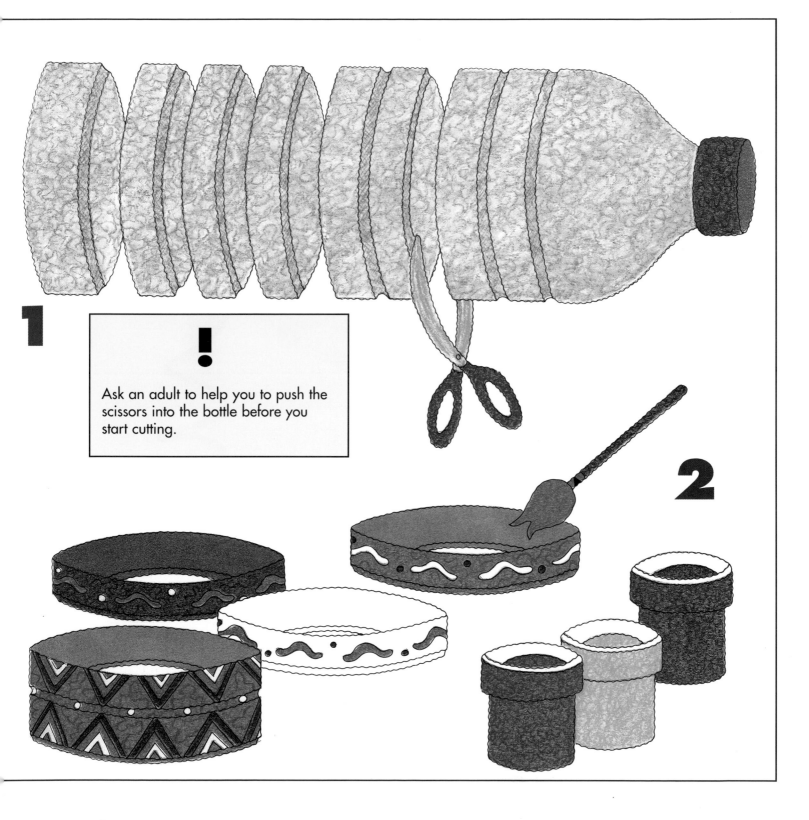

1

!

Ask an adult to help you to push the scissors into the bottle before you start cutting.

2

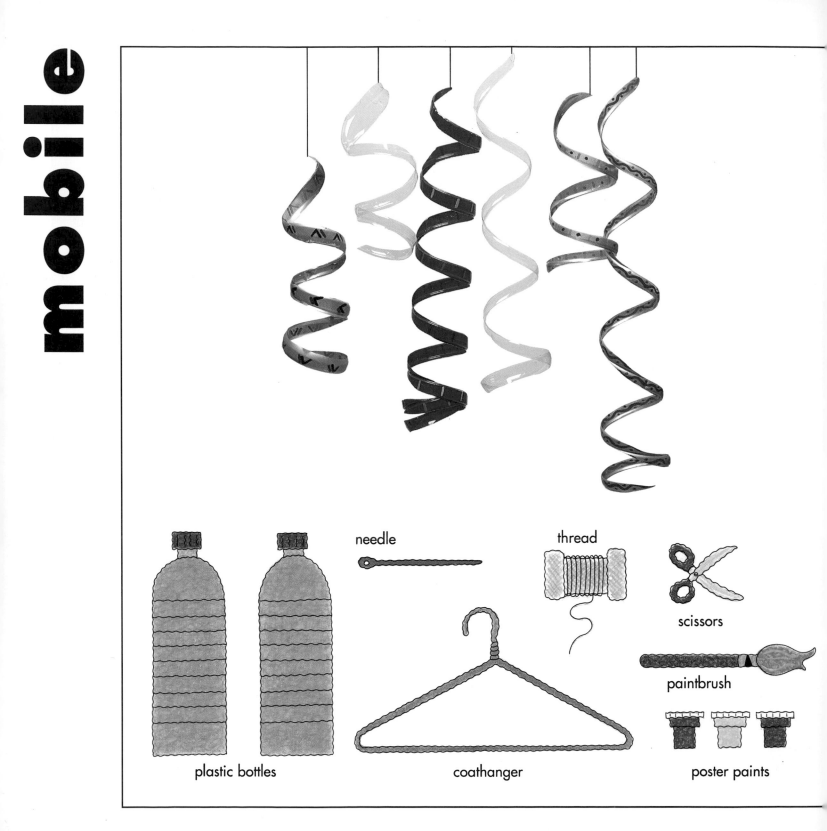

mobile

needle

thread

scissors

paintbrush

plastic bottles

coathanger

poster paints

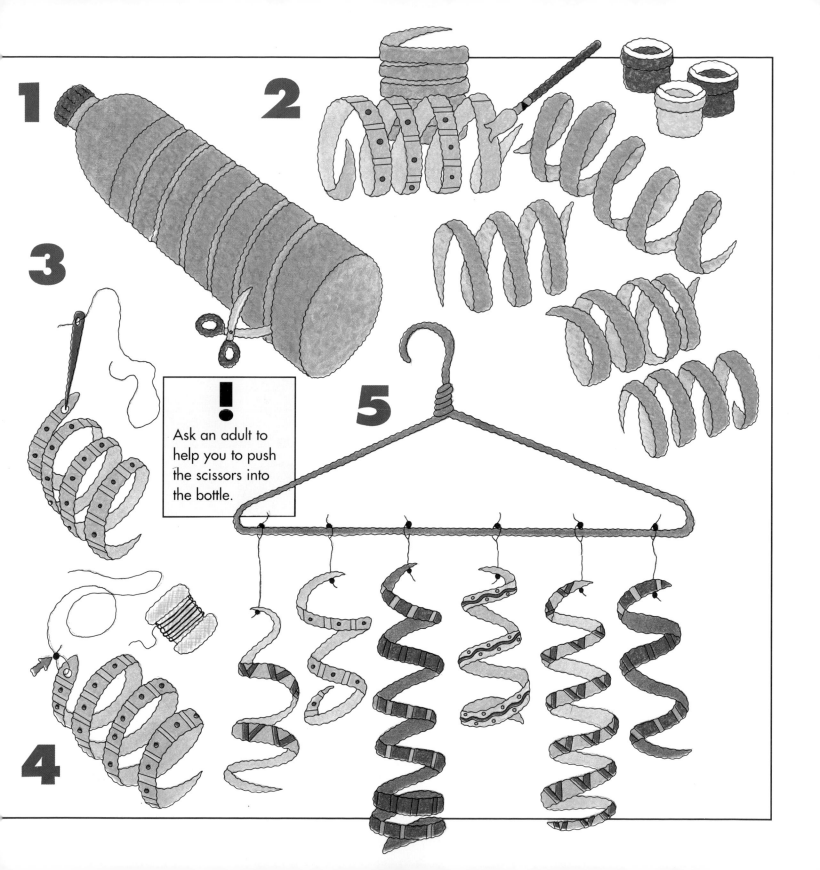

1

2

3

5

!

Ask an adult to
help you to push
the scissors into
the bottle.

4

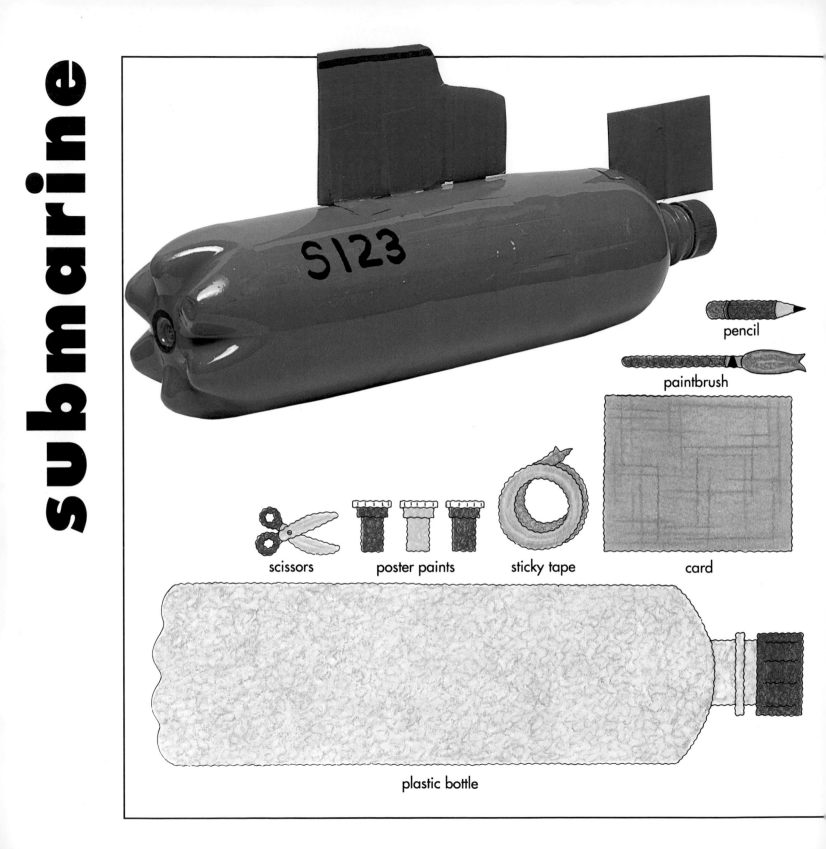

submarine

S123

pencil

paintbrush

scissors

poster paints

sticky tape

card

plastic bottle

1

2

3

!

Ask an adult to help you to cut the slits for the two fins.

4

S123

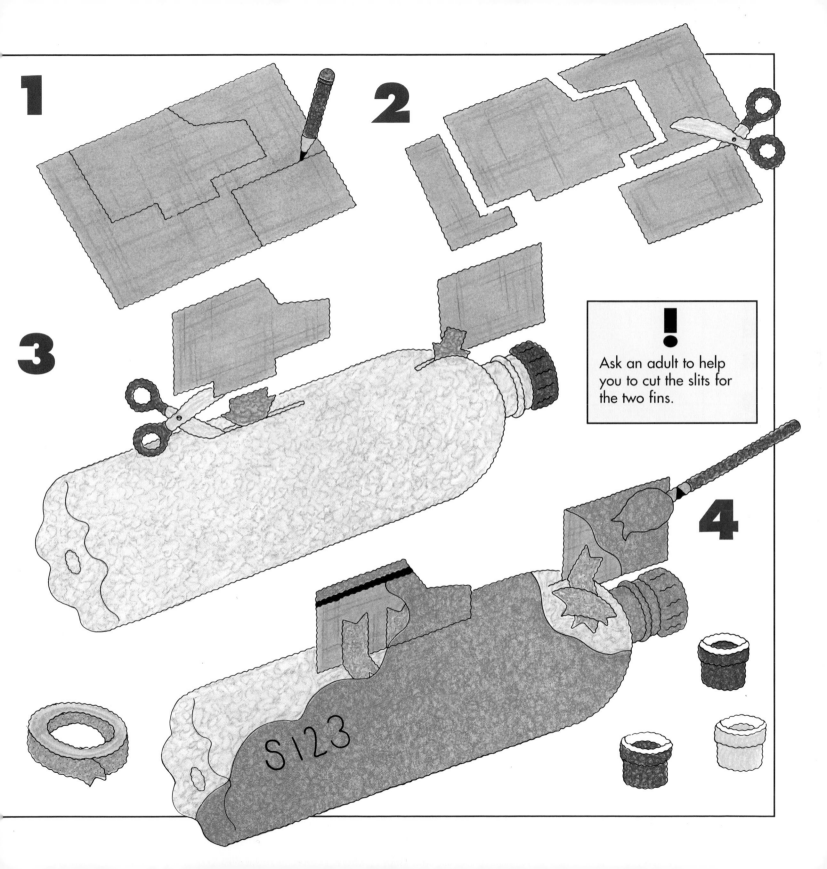

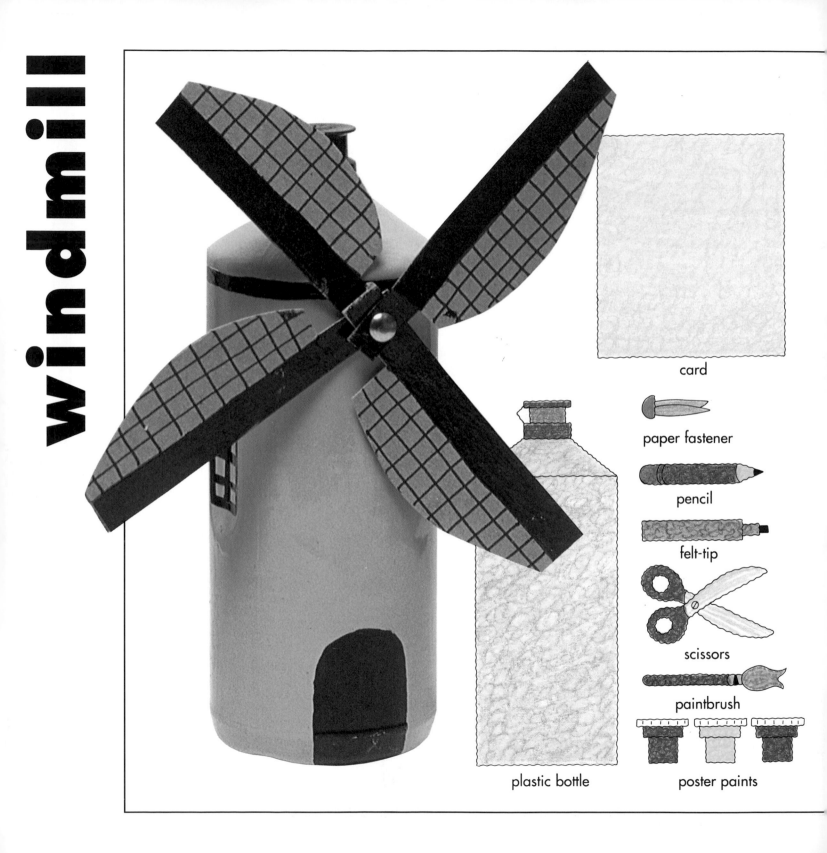

windmill

card

paper fastener

pencil

felt-tip

scissors

paintbrush

plastic bottle

poster paints

catamaran

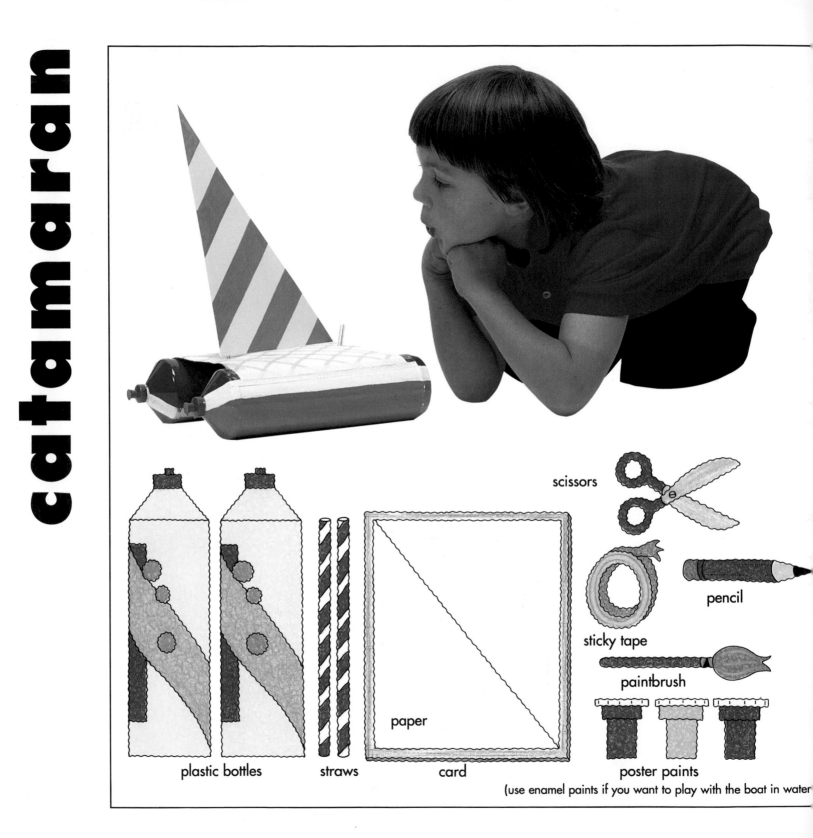

scissors

pencil

sticky tape

paintbrush

paper

plastic bottles

straws

card

poster paints

(use enamel paints if you want to play with the boat in water)

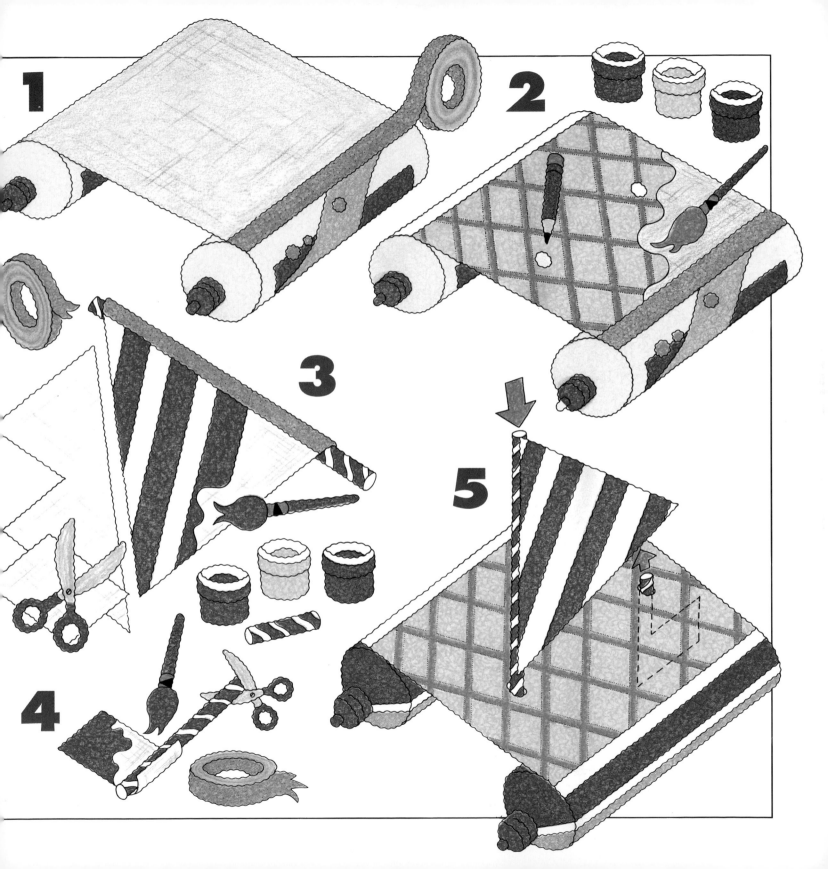

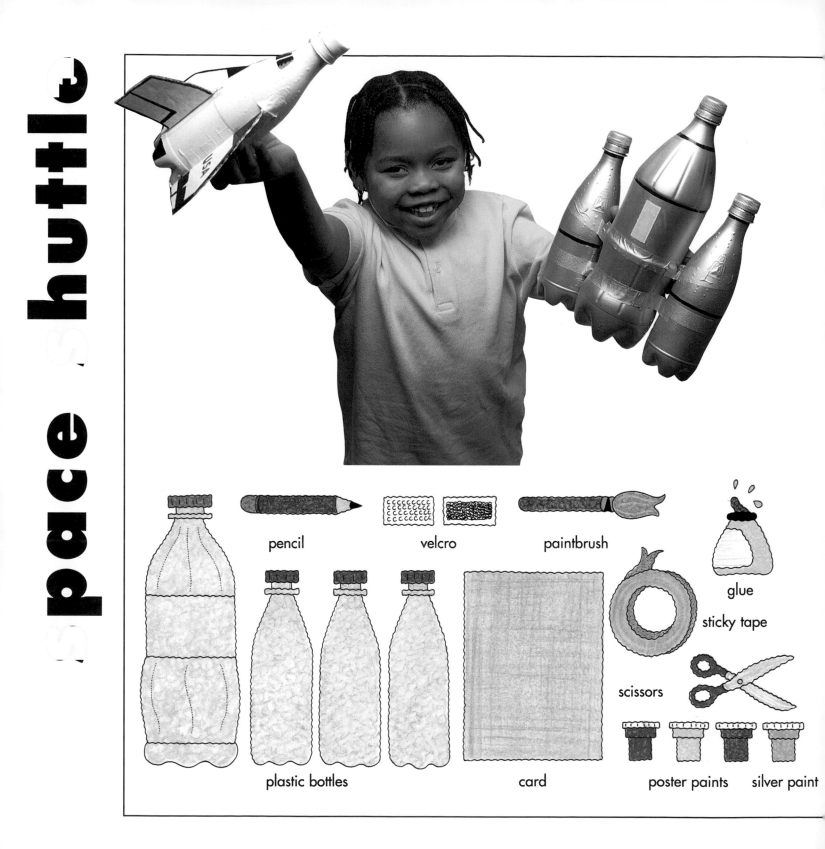

space shuttle

pencil

velcro

paintbrush

glue

sticky tape

scissors

plastic bottles

card

poster paints

silver paint

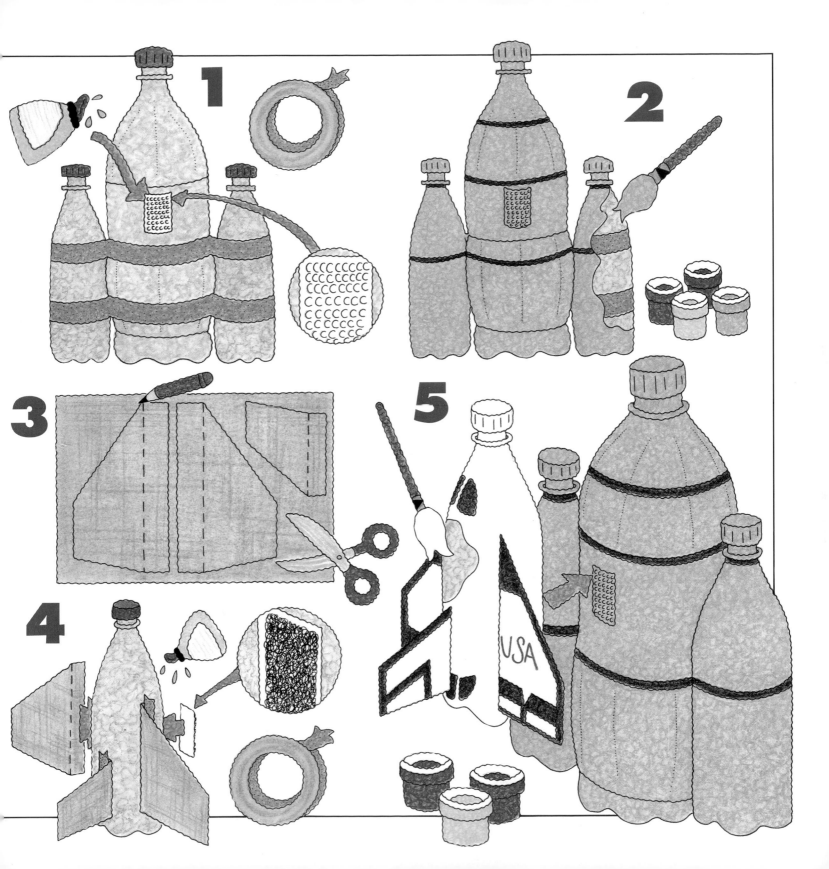

1

2

3

4

5

USA

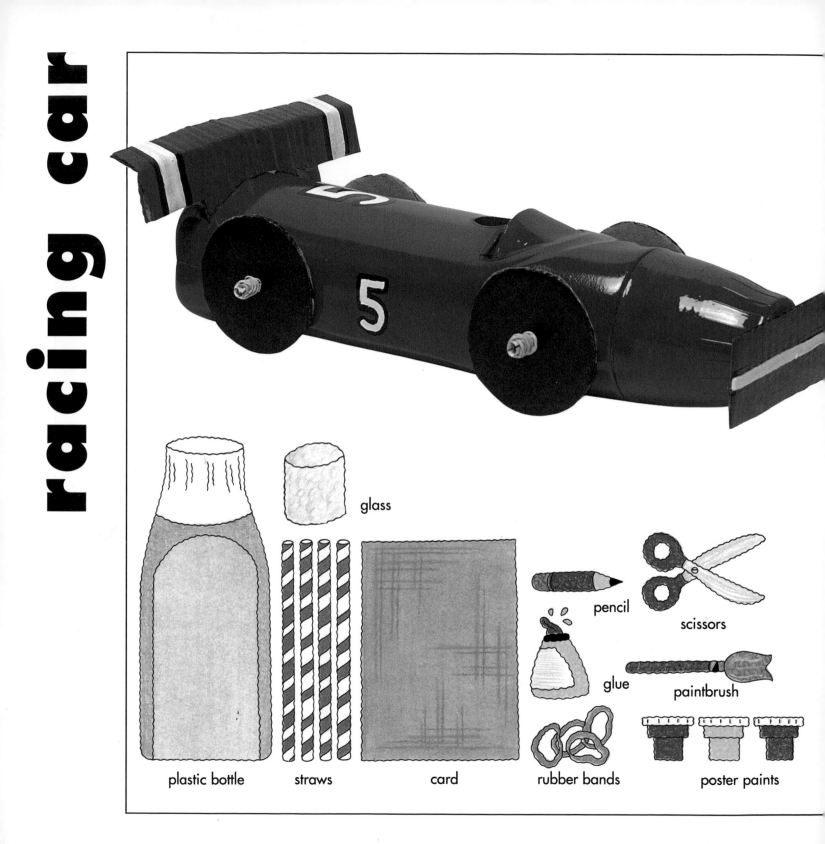

racing car

glass

pencil

scissors

glue

paintbrush

plastic bottle

straws

card

rubber bands

poster paints

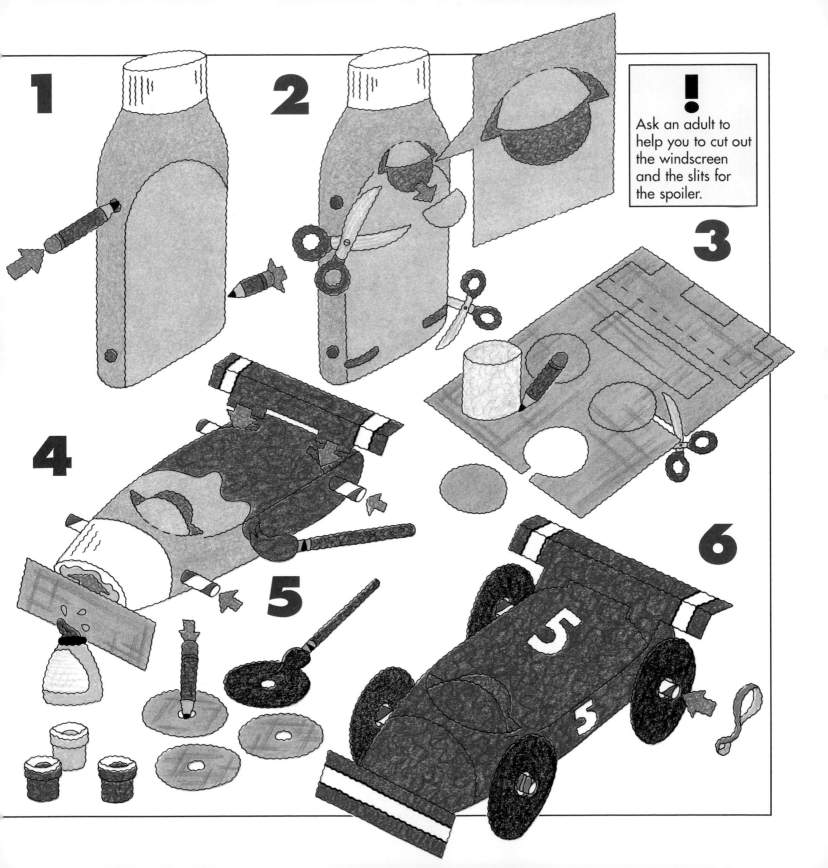

1

2

! Ask an adult to help you to cut out the windscreen and the slits for the spoiler.

3

4

5

6

colour chart

You can mix the three primary colours to make all the colours of the rainbow. Follow the chart below to mix the colours you want. The numbers on the pots show the proportions of each colour you need to make the new colour.

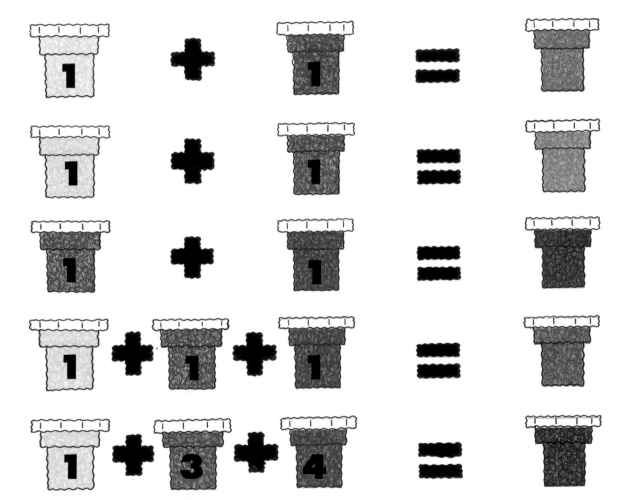

Different types of paint will give different results. Experiment by mixing different proportions of colours. Make sure you wash the brush before dipping it into each paint pot.